# A Day in the Life of a
# PENGUIN
## A 4D BOOK

by Sharon Katz Cooper

Consultant: Robert T. Mason
Professor of Integrative Biology
J.C. Braly Curator of Vertebrates
Oregon State University

**Download the Capstone 4D app!**

- Ask an adult to download the Capstone 4D app.
- Scan the cover and stars inside the book for additional content.

When you scan a spread, you'll find
fun extra stuff to go with this book!
You can also find these things
on the web at www.capstone4D.com
using the password: penguin.15176

A+ Books are published by Pebble
1710 Roe Crest Drive, North Mankato, Minnesota 56003
www.mycapstone.com

**Library of Congress Cataloging-in-Publication Data**
Names: Katz Cooper, Sharon, author.
Title: A day in the life of a penguin : a 4D book / by Sharon Katz Cooper.
Description: North Mankato, Minnesota : an imprint of Pebble, [2019] |
   Series: A+ books. A day in the life | Audience: Age 4–8.
Identifiers: LCCN 2018006121 (print) | LCCN 2018009146 (ebook) |
   ISBN 9781543515251 (eBook PDF) | ISBN 9781543515176 (library binding) |
   ISBN 9781543515213 (paperback)
Subjects: LCSH: Penguins—Life cycles—Juvenile literature.
Classification: LCC QL696.S47 (ebook) | LCC QL696.S47 K38 2019 (print) |
   DDC 598.47156—dc23
LC record available at https://lccn.loc.gov/2018006121

**Editorial Credits**
Gina Kammer, editor; Jennifer Bergstrom, designer;
Morgan Walters, media researcher; Laura Manthe, production specialist

**Photo Credits**
Getty Images : Mint Images - Frans Lanting, bottom 20, Paul Nicklen, top 8; Newscom: Jonathan Carlile
imageBROKER, top 20, Kevin Schafer/NHPA/Photoshot, 7, Poelking, F./picture alliance / Arco Images G,
22, R. Linke/picture alliance / blickwinkel/R, 15; Shutterstock: Alexey Seafarer, top 16, Andreea Dragomir, 4,
Dmytro Pylypenko, bottom 8, Lemberg Vector studio, Cover, design element throughout, Mario_Hoppmann,
26, MZPHOTO.CZ, 9, polarman, 27, Roger Clark ARPS, 1, 14, 18, 30, Sergey 402, 11, 13, bottom 16, 17,
TravelMediaProductions, 5, 6, vladsilver, Cover, 12, 19, 21, 23, 25; SuperStock: M. Watsonantheo / Pantheon, 29

## Note to Parents, Teachers, and Librarians

This book uses full color photographs and a nonfiction format to introduce the concept of a penguin's day.
*A Day in the Life of a Penguin* is designed to be read aloud to a pre-reader or to be read independently by
an early reader. Photographs help listeners and early readers understand the text and concepts discussed.
The book encourages further learning by including the following sections: Table of Contents, Glossary,
Read More, Internet Sites, Critical Thinking Questions, and Index. Early readers may need assistance
using these features.

Printed in the United States of America.
PA017

# TABLE OF CONTENTS

# A Penguin's Day

The cold morning wind blows. Waves hit the Antarctic ice. The emperor penguin opens her eyes. She flaps her short black wings. She is a bird, but penguins don't fly.

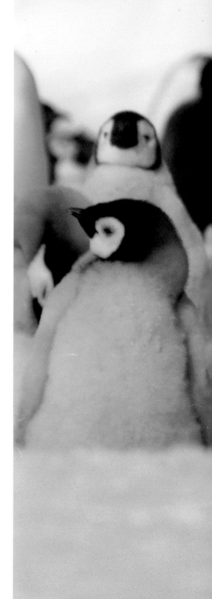

It's time to find some breakfast. *SWISH!*
The penguin slides on her white belly.
She gets to the edge of the ice.

SWISH!

*SPLASH!* She belly-flops into icy water. Her thick layer of fat under her feathers is her coat. It keeps her warm. Her short wings are like paddles. The penguin looks like she's flying under the water! Right, left, right, left, she chases fish until she catches one. She snaps it up in her strong beak. *GULP!*

All morning the penguin catches fish. She also eats squid and krill. She dives very deep. She stays underwater for 5 to 6 minutes. She can stay underwater for as long as 18 minutes!

KRILL!

As the penguin hunts, she watches for leopard seals and killer whales. These predators are animals that would try to eat HER for lunch.

Now it's time for the penguin to go back to the colony. The colony is a large group of penguins that live together. She jumps her 80-pound (36-kilogram), 4-foot (122-centimeter) tall body out of the water. She slides up onto the ice. Then she waddles back to her group. Sometimes she slides on her belly. That's a faster way to travel!

*WUH-OO-OO, WUH-OO-OO!* What's making that sound? Fuzzy, gray penguin chicks! Each penguin chick makes its own song. The penguin follows the song to her baby.

The chick snuggles next to the penguin's
mate. The penguin's mate is her male partner.
He is the chick's father. He kept the chick warm
while the penguin looked for food.

SNUGGLE!

The penguin puts her beak into the chick's throat. She pushes food from her own stomach to her chick. Her breakfast is her baby's breakfast too!

FOOD!

A large bird lands nearby. The bird wants to eat the chick. *CA-AH! CA-AH!* it cries. The penguin's mate sees it. He snaps his beak. He flaps his wings. The bird flies away. The chick is safe.

FLAP!

The penguin's mate goes to the water to hunt. The penguin stays and snuggles close to the chick.

The penguin's mate comes back. The little penguin family is all together! The parents take turns feeding and warming their chick.

Keeping the chick warm is very important. The chick does not yet have a full layer of fat. The fat would help it stay warm.

WARM!

The penguin and her mate must protect the chick from the cold. If they don't, it could die.

The penguin has warm feet. Her feet have layers of fat. Her feet also have strong claws. They grab onto the ice. The chick sits on the top of the penguin's feet sometimes. It uses them like a tiny rug.

GRAB!

Every few hours the chick wanders off. It plays with
other penguin chicks. But it never goes too far away.

While the penguin and her mate look for fish, their chick stays behind. It stands with other chicks in groups called crèches. No babysitter is needed! The chicks stay close to each other to keep warm.

The wind still blows cold. The day has been long. The penguin squeezes closer together with other penguins. This helps all the penguins keep warm.

She takes a turn close to the center of the group. It is warmest there. After a while, she moves to the outside. Other penguins get a turn in the middle.

It's the end of the day in the penguin colony. The penguin tucks her chick between her feet. She stands close to her mate. She closes her eyes. She will try to get some sleep.

## Good night, penguin!

# LIFE CYCLE OF AN
# EMPEROR PENGUIN

**1**
Penguins begin life as **EGGS.** The father penguin keeps the egg warm on top of his feet.

**2**
The chick hatches out after **65** to **75** days.

**3**
The mother penguin returns from hunting and takes a turn **FEEDING** the chick. The father goes off to feed.

**4**
When the father returns, he and the mother penguin **TAKE TURNS** feeding the chick.

**5**
As the season warms up, the chick learns how to **CATCH FISH** on its own.

**6**
After one year, the chick is close to the same size as its parents. It is almost ready to **FIND A MATE** of its own.

# Glossary

**colony**—a large group of penguins that live together

**crèche (KRESH)**—a group of young penguin chicks

**krill**—a small, shrimp-like animal

**leopard seal**—a large, spotted mammal that lives in the water and on ice

**mate**—the male or female partner for a penguin

**predator**—an animal that hunts other animals for food

**squid**—a sea animal with a long, soft body

# Read More

**De Silva, Kay.** *Penguins: Amazing Pictures & Fun Facts on Animals in Nature.* Our Amazing World Series. CreateSpace Independent Publishing Platform, 2015.

**Evans, Janet.** *Penguins: 101 Fun Facts & Amazing Pictures.* Speedy Publishing, 2015.

**Schuh, Mari.** *Penguins.* Black and White Animals. North Mankato, Minn.: Capstone Press, 2017.

# Internet Sites

Use FactHound to find Internet sites related to this book.

Visit *www.facthound.com*

Just type in 9781543515176 and go.

Check out projects, games and lots more at **www.capstonekids.com**

# Critical Thinking Questions

1. Why do you think emperor penguins have only one chick at a time?

2. What does an adult penguin eat? What does a baby penguin eat?

3. How do you think the penguins are able to recognize their family members?

4. Why do you think the center of the penguin colony is the warmest spot?

# Index